W e hope this Leaders Guide, with full text of DVD talks, pastoral notes on the series and prayers by Celia Bowring, will help and equip you if you are a church or group leader, or following *Finishingline* as an individual.

The DVDs are presented by John Wyatt, with introductions by Philippa Taylor.

Professor John Wyatt has worked as a consultant neonatologist at University College Hospital for more than twenty years, but is now concentrating on teaching and research into ethical dilemmas raised by advances in technology. He is past Chair of the Medical Study Group of the Christian Medical Fellowship (CMF) and a board member of Biocentre. His book *Matters of Life and Death* is published by IVP.

Philippa Taylor is Head of Public Policy at the Christian Medical Fellowship and is also a Consultant to CARE on bioethics and family issues. She has an MA in Bioethics, and for the past twenty years has been speaking, writing and working on a range of contemporary bioethical issues. She is also a competitive runner.

Celia Bowring is prayer coordinator for CARE and has written the CARE *Prayer Diary* for over thirty years. Married to Lyndon Bowring, Executive Chairman of CARE, she is also a speaker and writer.

Contents

Preface

For many of us, everyday life is often characterised by efforts to stave off the ageing process. Diets, lifestyle, vitamins, exercise, replacement organs - it's a major industry, as Bryan Appleyard points out in his book, *How to live forever or die trying!* And the sociologist Zygmunt Bauman has suggested that this medicalisation of daily life represents the primary strategy of modern times for suppressing the fear of death. For most people, death is a terrifying prospect.

There's no doubt that the Christian community has much to contribute to the theme of death and dying, and it is important that we speak up. Some of the most substantial challenges to the Christian faith today relate to the question of our human identity. On several significant fronts – whether human sexuality, transhumanism, or beginning- and end-of-life issues – the biblical view of humankind needs to be defended, explained and modelled in the public arena. John Wyatt's contribution to the area of medical ethics is well known, and

this study course on death and dying is welcome and timely.

At the same time as the London Olympics, the Keswick Convention ran a three week event on the theme of Going the Distance – living the Christian life in the light of eternity. John Wyatt's compassionate and insightful lecture on the subject of this study guide was an outstanding part of that theme, and is the reason why Keswick Ministries is honoured to support *Finishing Line*, together with CARE.

Dag Hammarskjold once said that no philosophy that cannot make sense of death can make sense of life either. Christians, therefore, have the opportunity, by personal example and compassionate care, to show the world what it means to die well, and therefore to live well. Jim Packer once suggested that the Christian should approach death in the same way as children prepare for a summer holiday – packed up and ready to go, well in advance! This study guide will help us to do that, and help others to do the same.

Jonathan Lamb
CEO and Minister-at-large for Keswick Ministries. Vice President of International Federation of Evangelical Students

Foreword

What a great privilege it is for CARE to have worked alongside Keswick Ministries and Professor John Wyatt to produce this unique resource. It's designed especially for small groups - where Christians can get to know each other enough to discuss and pray over this sensitive issue that is very likely to touch hearts and challenge faith. I can think of nobody better than John to help us address the topics of assisted suicide, euthanasia, the value of every human life and what the Bible teaches us about dying well. He has a true pastor's heart, a deep understanding and love of Scripture and the medical knowledge and experience needed to guide us through these important ethical and personal matters. These qualities come out so well in his introductory DVD talks before each section, and it is also particularly fitting that Philippa Taylor, CARE's bioethics consultant, joins John in these talks.

I believe that *Finishing Line* will bring clarity to the minds, and comfort for the emotions of those who watch the DVD talks and work through the study booklets. These are matters of life and death, and they're inescapable. I am confident that this resource will be a positive resource that many church leaders will wish to use.

Lyndon Bowring
Executive Chairman, CARE

Introduction

The primary aim of this five part project is to enable Christian believers to explore difficult, important and personal questions about death and dying from the perspective of the historic biblical Christian faith. However, these discussion sessions may also be appropriate for those who are not believers but who are interested in the topic. Experience has shown that many people are interested and concerned about the issues of assisted suicide, euthanasia and dying well, and these topics sometimes provide a 'way in' to exploration of the faith for those who are not open to more conventional forms of evangelism.

It is never easy to talk about death. So the group may require sensitive, gentle and encouraging leadership, and a preparedness to share honestly about our own anxieties and vulnerabilities.

However, as Christian believers we do not need to share in the fears and despair of those in our society who have no hope. As people who are changed by the Easter message, we know that death is a defeated enemy. And the truth is that dying well need not be all loss – in fact it can be a time of opportunity and internal growth, even a strange and wonderful adventure.

So our hope and prayer is that the discussions would not only be challenging but also a source of practical encouragement and spiritual hope. There are no easy answers but dying need not be a totally negative subject. There are spiritual, human and medical resources to support us on this journey, and the aim of the group leader should be to enable these issues to be addressed in a compassionate, biblical and informative way.

As a leader, it will obviously be important to know something about the personal and faith background of the group members, and you may need to help to orientate and frame the discussion in a way which is relevant to them.

Each of the five discussion sessions are structured in the same way:

1 A brief introduction and welcome from the local group leader.

2 DVD - a short introduction from Philippa Taylor to set the scene.

3 DVD – a talk from John Wyatt lasting about ten minutes.

4 Discussion based on the questions, Bible verses and quotations in the booklet. This can be of variable length but probably not more than an hour.

5 The group leader sums up the discussion, points to further material and resources in the booklet, reminds members about the timing and topic of the next discussion in the series and closes with prayer – possibly using Celia Bowring's prayers at the end of each session.

Notes --

Group dynamics

Death and dying are not easy topics for discussion, particularly if we are asked to talk about what the process of dying might involve for us and for our loved ones. It is a subject that can raise uneasy questions and anxieties, reminding us of our own frailty and vulnerability. As some group members might be feeling apprehensive about the topics for discussion, it is important that the group leader verbalises these concerns and helps to put people at ease from the beginning.

The aim should be to provide a safe, open and non-judgemental atmosphere in which opinions and anxieties can be expressed openly without fear of criticism or condemnation. It is inevitable that some group members will bring their own personal experiences of the deaths of family members and close friends into the discussion. Some may have witnessed traumatic and unpleasant events which have left them confused or anxious.

The group leader should enable members' own experiences to be expressed where appropriate, but should try to prevent one person's experiences from having a dominant influence on the discussion.

When addressing a particular question the group leader should have further questions in mind to help to develop an initial answer. 'What did you mean by that?', 'Can you say a bit more?', 'What does everyone else think?'

If someone gives an answer that appears to be unhelpful or that is leading the group in an unproductive direction, tact and gentleness may be required to steer the discussion tactfully back to the topic. One way could be to focus on one or two of the Bible verses, and ask members to reflect on the verse and its relevance to the main topic of the evening.

Sometimes, individual personalities may make the group dynamics difficult:

The silent person: This person almost never contributes to the discussion. He or she may be best helped by forming groups of two or three and then having them feed their answers to the main group. However, don't interpret silence to mean that the person is disengaged. Some people are more comfortable and learn more from listening rather than active contribution.

The talkative person: This person likes to monopolize the discussion. You may find it helpful to divide into smaller groups to give others an opportunity to speak. Alternatively a quiet word in private may be helpful, for example, 'Tim. Thanks so much for everything you are

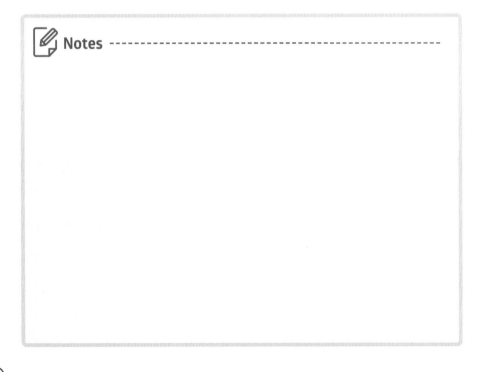

Notes --

contributing. I wonder if you could help me with the quieter members of the group...'

The arguer: This person tends to attack or ridicule the answers given by other members of the group. It is important to recognise that this person may be speaking out of their own experiences of pain or rejection, and hence not to take their contributions at face value. It may be helpful to listen to any specific issue that they may have – after the main meeting. If it seems appropriate, one-to-one pastoral support may be helpful.

The know-it-all: This person tends to answer every question immediately, in a way that stifles the group discussion. You might need to add supplementary questions to other members of the group, for example, 'Does everybody agree with Nick?', 'What do you think about that Sarah?'

The off-at-an-angle person: This person tends to steer the discussion away from the topic into an entirely different direction. It may be helpful to bring the group back to the question being discussed and tactfully suggest that the new topic could be discussed after the meeting.

Summarising and closing the discussion at the end of a session

It is helpful for the group leader to sum up the discussion, highlighting particular points that seem to be most productive, possibly pointing to further material and resources in the booklet and elsewhere. If significant differences have emerged, it may be helpful to emphasise that these are difficult and painful topics and that there are no simplistic answers to many deep questions. Encourage group members to stay with the course and remind them about the time and the topic of the next discussion in the series. It may be appropriate to have a time of open prayer and reflection, or the leader may close with a short prayer.

1

Euthanasia and Medically Assisted Suicide – the current scene

----

This session focuses on the wide public support and political lobbying for a change in the law to allow euthanasia and physician assisted suicide. Why have these topics become so prominent in today's culture? The aim of this session is to help group members to recognise the force of the arguments in favour of changing the law to allow euthanasia and assisted suicide, and to identify the personal fears and deep spiritual issues that lie behind the public debates.

📖 Text of the talk

'This is the first in a series of group discussions on issues around death and dying in the modern world. In today's discussion we will be concentrating on the wide public support and political lobbying for a change in the law to allow physician assisted suicide. Why have these topics become so prominent in today's culture? In this introductory talk I will be raising a number of questions and topics for discussion.

Future sessions will look at a Christian and biblical understanding of what it means to be human; the third session will examine the topic of suicide in more detail, asking whether this can ever be a godly way to die, and then the final two sessions will look at positive alternatives, what does it mean in reality to die well and to die faithfully – and what steps can we take now to prepare for this.

God's image

It is never easy to talk about death, particularly about our own mortality. But as Christian people we do not need to share in the terrible fears and despair of those in our society who have no hope. As people who are changed by the Easter message we know that death is a defeated enemy. In fact, in the language of the New Testament Christian believers do not die, they "fall asleep", in the hope of the resurrection and of meeting face to face the One who cries, "Behold I make all things new".

Here are the words of Martin Amis, the novelist. "There should be a way out for rational people who have decided they are in the negative. That should be available and it should be easy. There should

> 'You matter because you are you, and you matter to the end of your life. Not only will we help you die with dignity but we will help you to live before you die.'
> Cicely Saunders

📝 Notes

be a booth on every corner where you could get a martini and a medal."

The words were deliberately flippant, but Martin Amis was deadly serious. He had seen the protracted death of loved-ones at close quarters and he didn't want to go in the same way. Many other celebrities and media personalities have joined the chorus calling for the legalisation of physician assisted suicide.

Media coverage

Then there is the steady stream of despairing suicides who make the journey to the Dignitas clinic in Zurich, like the elderly and frail conductor Sir Edwards Downes. His wife had cancer, and they had made a suicide pact - they would die together - and so supported by their children they travelled to Switzerland where hand in hand they took a lethal concoction of drugs together. The media comments were almost entirely positive. What a noble and responsible way to go. And why on earth did they have to travel to Switzerland – why couldn't they take the lethal drugs here in the UK?

Another case is that of the GP Anne Turner. She had nursed her husband with a degenerative neurological condition until his death. Then to her horror she detected the first signs of a similar degenerative condition in herself. She took some tablets and attempted suicide but unsuccessfully. Then she persuaded her family, "If you really love me you'll help me to die by taking me to the Dignitas clinic." At first they were horrified and attempted to talk her out of it. But eventually they came round. As the newspaper headline put it, "Anne Turner sang songs and joked with her children – then she went to a clinic to die".

Then there was the tragic case of the young rugby player Daniel James. He was a very talented player – he had played for the English junior team. Then he was involved in a horrific rugby accident, sustained a fracture of the neck with spinal cord damage and became permanently paralysed from the chest downwards. He became depressed and then he was suicidal. He persuaded his parents eventually to take him to the Dignitas clinic. And there he took the tablets and died. The widespread media coverage was again largely supportive. What loving parents they were to sacrifice their own interests for the best interests of their child.

Another recent case is that of Tony Nicklinson. He had the rare and devastating condition of "locked-in syndrome", following a stroke. He was fully conscious but unable to move any muscles except for blinking, which he used to communicate through a computer. He argued that his life was pointless and if he had any useful muscle movement he would have commited suicide already. So his argument was that a doctor should be allowed to kill him at his request with lethal drugs.

Personal involvement

At present in the UK, although suicide itself is not illegal, assisting someone else to commit suicide is a serious criminal offence. Yet in a range of surveys, over 80 per cent of the UK population support a change in the law to allow people to kill themselves with a doctor's help. In Holland, where euthanasia of people dying from terminal illness is

> 'Hope is to hear the melody of the future: Faith is to dance to that melody in the present.'
> Anon

now a routine procedure, there is now an active campaign to extend euthanasia or mercy killing to three groups of people, first those with severe permanent psychiatric distress, then those with early signs of dementia, and finally those who are merely "tired of life"….

So here are some important philosophical and theological issues. But they are also issues of human pain. Whenever we discuss these complex and difficult topics I think our first responsibility as Christians is to empathise with many people in our society who feel that life is not worth living. We must try to understand the deep internal pain that drives them to wish to end their lives. We must talk about these issues not with judgement or fear in voices – but with tears in our eyes.

Notes

Secondly, they are not just issues out there in society – they are in here, in this room. I don't know who is watching this video but I can guarantee that many people who are watching are personally involved with these issues. Maybe you have watched a loved one, a parent or a spouse, struggle with terminal illness, or with dementia, and you have wondered whether death would not be preferable to prolonged survival. Or perhaps you yourself know that you have a condition which is likely to lead to your own death and you are wondering what the future holds.

We are all involved in one way or another. These are not just problems out there in society, they touch all of us, because of our common humanity. But why is it that at this time in our history, debates about the legalisation of medical killing have become so prominent? What are the social, personal and spiritual forces that lie behind this debate? Many modern people find it inconceivable that they are not allowed to control the timing and the manner of their death. If I can control every other aspect of my life, if my right to choose is central to my existence, then why on earth can I not choose and control the way in which I die?

Legal safeguards

For more than a thousand years suicide has been opposed in all Western countries. But now there are increasing voices arguing that suicide can be noble,

responsible, even a godly way to die. And it is argued that it is the duty of society and of the medical profession to come up with a formal system, with legal safeguards to allow people to kill themselves.

I think that the desire to control death for many people is driven by fear. Perhaps it is fear of suffering, or fear of medical over-treatment, or fear of becoming dependent on others.

You know as Christians approaching the finishing line, it doesn't have to be like this. Now there is an opportunity to discuss some of these complex and painful issues together.

I hope that you will join me in future sessions where we will look at biblical responses, the Christian hope and what it means to die well and to die faithfully.'

$Q1$ **What do you think are the personal fears and desires** which lie behind the support for the legalisation of euthanasia and medically assisted suicide? Do any of these resonate with you?

These include the fear of suffering and pain, the fear of indignity, the fear of medical overtreatment and the fear of dependence. Issues concerning the widespread fear of dependence are of particular significance.

$Q2$ **Why do you think euthanasia is supported by many journalists and opinion formers?**

Euthanasia and assisted suicide resonates with modern preoccupations with individualism and the right to direct their own life. Modern people demand the right to control the timing and the manner of their death.

$Q3$ **Why do you think this issue has become so prominent at this point in Western culture and society? What spiritual issues and trends lie at the root of these fears and desires?**

Spiritual issues include first, resistance to the idea that human beings are created to be dependent on one another and on God. Second, there is the idea that all moral values are relative – if I decide that it is right to kill myself, who are you to question me? Third is the idea that medical technology can provide a solution to the age-old problems of humanity.

$Q4$ **What do you think might be some of the practical risks for individuals and also for society if euthanasia and/or medically assisted suicide were to be legalised? In what ways might it affect us individually and personally?**

Risks include a) the possibility that the diagnosis of a terminal illness is incorrect – this is not uncommon in medical practice; b) methods of medical killing may go wrong, leading to an individual who survives but with greater disability; c) vulnerable individuals may feel a covert pressure to request medical killing in order to benefit their relatives and others; d) involvement in medical killing may affect doctors and other health professionals leading to less respect for human life; e) difficult cases may lead to a gradual extension in the legal grounds for medical killing.

Bible passages for reflection

Hebrews 2:14,15

'Since therefore the children share in flesh and blood, he himself likewise partook of the same things, that through death he might destroy the one who has the power of death, that is, the devil, and deliver all those who through fear of death were subject to lifelong slavery.'

Fear of death is a powerful force that leads to lifelong slavery. The devil is the one who has the power of death, but he has been destroyed by the death of Jesus Christ, who shared in our humanity.

Hebrews 9:27

'Just as it is appointed for man to die once, and after that comes judgement.'

The awesome nature of death is seen in that it only occurs once, but it is followed by personal judgement. Those who are believers in Christ need not face death with fear, since he has paid the penalty for our sins.

Ecclesiastes 9:5,6

'For the living know that they will die, but the dead know nothing, and they have no more reward, for the memory of them is forgotten. Their love and their hate and their envy have already perished, and forever they have no more share in all that is done under the sun.'

This text illustrates a human response to death from the perspective of one who has no knowledge of eternal life beyond the grave.

John 11:25

'Jesus said to her, "I am the resurrection and the life. Whoever believes in me, though he die, yet shall he live, and everyone who lives and believes in me shall never die. Do you believe this?"'

Believers in Jesus can trust in the resurrection life which he will give to us after our bodily death. The words of Jesus challenge us individually as to whether we are prepared personally to commit ourselves to this belief in our bodily resurrection.

Notes

 ## Closing Prayer

Almighty God, we worship You as the Lord of all Life – Creator, Redeemer and the Judge of us all. We pray about general public opinion and for politicians, medical professional and the media to understand the significance and dangers of changing the law to allow physician assisted dying or any other form of euthanasia. Amen.

 Notes --

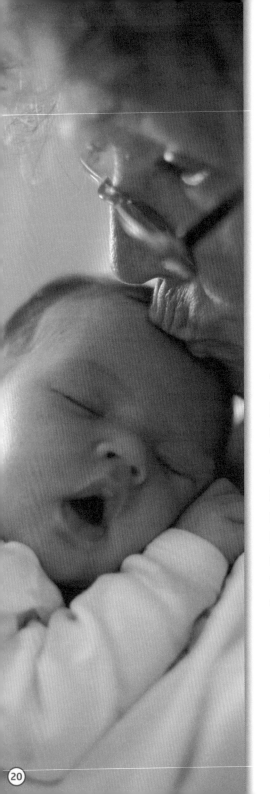

2
What does it mean to be human?

In this session we will be concentrating on the Bible's teaching about what it means to be human. We are created in God's image – as wonderful, mysterious and unique beings. But in God's creation plans it seems that we are also designed to be fragile, frail, vulnerable and dependent.

🗣️ Text of the talk

Being human

'This is the second in a series of group discussions on issues around death and dying in the modern world. In today's discussion we will be concentrating on what the Bible teaches about what it means to be human. Because the truth is that the question of what it means to be human lies of the heart of modern debates about death and dying. If we are merely biological machines, the meaningless product of chance and scientific laws, then choosing to destroy our lives in an act of suicide might seem an appropriate thing to do, even responsible. But the Bible gives us a very different picture.

Here are three foundations of the biblical view.

First of all Genesis 1:27. At the climax of the creation account in Genesis 1, human beings are unique in all the vast array of created beings because they alone, male and female, are created in God's image. Wonderfully and mysteriously, each one of us has been created to reflect God's being and character. Each one of us is unique, created to know God, with an eternal meaning and destiny. Human beings are God-like beings. All human life is special and so in a strange way the destruction of a human life is in some way a profound insult to God himself.

> '...earth to earth, ashes to ashes, dust to dust; in sure and certain hope of the resurrection to eternal life, through our Lord Jesus Christ...'.
> Book of Common Prayer

Secondly, the Creator's mysterious plan was to take this amazing God-like image and place it in a pathetic, fragile, vulnerable, physical body. So in the parallel creation narrative in Genesis 2, human beings are said to be created out of the dust of the ground. Adam, the Hebrew for mankind, is derived from adamah - the ground. And in English the word "human" is derived from "humus", not the nice dip you put on pitta bread but the compost heap! So God has chosen in creation to make us out of dust, out of the same stuff as everything else. And therefore we are designed to share the weakness, vulnerability and dependence of the rest of the physical creation. Presumably God could have chosen to make us differently. He could have made us strong, resilient, powerful and independent – but instead he chose to make us weak, fragile and vulnerable.

Total dependence

So dependence is not an alien, subhuman, undignified condition. No, it is part of the narrative of every human life. You came into this world utterly and totally dependent on the love and care of others – you could do nothing for yourself but somebody cared for you, somebody loved you, somebody fed you - and we go through a phase of life when other people depend on us, and then most of us will end our lives totally dependent on the love and care of others.

I learnt this is in a vivid way from the experience of caring for my mother. Grace was a lovely vivacious person of deep compassion and Christian vision, but then she was struck down by a horrible and progressive form of neurological illness. She became confused, she was hallucinating, disorientated. Eventually she could do nothing for herself – she was totally dependent on 24-hour nursing care. Near the end I was visiting her and somebody thrust a yoghurt pot and a teaspoon into my hand. I was trying to feed her, "Here it comes, open your mouth, open your mouth…" And then I had a sudden flashback. This is precisely what she used to say to me – I could remember her saying it but now the tables were turned. And I remember at the time thinking, "This is the way it was meant to be". I was learning more of what it meant to be a son and she was learning more of what it meant to be a mother. Because dependence is part of the story, it is part of the plan.

Thirdly, we were created in families so that we could care for one another. I often hear old people, including Christian

old people, who should know better, say something like – I just don't want to be a burden to anybody. I'm happy to care for other people, but I don't want to be looked after. I'd rather go to heaven than that.

If you ever hear someone say that you must immediately say, "You are wrong! – you are designed to be a burden. I am designed to be a burden to you and you are designed to be a burden to me."

To be a human being is to be called to share the burdens of the life which God has given us. The life of a family, including that of the local church – the Christian church family - should be one of "mutual burdensomeness".

 Notes --

But the Christian faith teaches us something even more wonderful and amazing. Because God himself, the Creator of the universe, breaks into the world. How? As a pathetic, vulnerable and totally dependent newborn baby. We are so familiar with the doctrine of the incarnation that we have lost its scandalous force. God makes himself a baby who can do absolutely nothing for himself, a fragile and wonderful being who depends on human breasts for milk and human hands to wipe his bottom. Jesus starts his life totally dependent on the love and care of others. And how does his earthly life come to a close? With arms and legs stretched on a cross and from his parched lips comes the words, "I am thirsty…".

Unique value

God chooses to make himself vulnerable and dependent. And yet even at these times of total dependence, the Bible teaches us that he was still the Second Person of the Trinity, upholding the universe by the word of his power. His divine status and dignity is in no way touched by his dependence. Please remember this if you find yourself in a place of total dependence and you have to rely on others to feed you and care for you and wash you. Your dependence in no way damages, changes or demeans your unique value, status and dignity as a precious and wonderful princess or prince of the Most High.

> **'I am designed to be a burden to you and you are designed to be a burden to me … And the life of a family, including that of the local church, should be one of 'mutual burdensomeness.'"**
> (from talk)

If dependence is good enough for Jesus then it's good enough for us. Jesus shares the created fragility of our humanity, and the narrative of a human life. In fact there is nothing that we can go through in the painful experiences of human life, including the experiences of dying, in which in some sense Jesus has not gone before us. As Gilbert Meilaender puts it, "Jesus was with us in the darkness of the womb, as he will be with us in the darkness of the tomb".

So, dependence is the way that God has made us – and yet the truth is that many of us, including me, struggle to accept this in reality. We would much prefer to live independent lives than to be someone who needs looking after, to be cared for. If God has made us dependent on others, why do we struggle to find this so hard to accept in practice?

Now there's a chance to reflect on some Bible passages and to discuss some questions which we've created to take these issues further.'

Q1 Why do many Christian believers fear the possibility of dependence or being a burden to others in old age? Why do you think that we find it so hard to accept caring from others? How would you feel if you became dependent on your family or other carers?

The reality of dependence challenges our belief that we are in control of own lives. Many of us find depending on others humiliating and demeaning to our sense of our 'self'. We may derive a sense of our own importance and value from caring from others, hence the inability to care for others robs us of a sense of importance. Dependence is something that may seem childlike and not appropriate for an adult.

Q2 To what extent is dependence part of our creation design as human beings, and to what extent part of our fallenness and our sinful nature? What is the biblical and other evidence to support this? Look particularly at Genesis 2:7, Psalm 103:13, 14 and Galatians 6:2. What positive value might there be in our human fragility, dependence and vulnerability?

The Biblical narrative consistently teaches that part of our created nature as human beings is dependence on one another and on God himself. Biblical passages include those referred to below, especially Genesis 2:7, Psalm 103:13,14 and Galatians 6:2. Other passages include Ecclesiastes 4:9-12, Psalm 22:9-11, and Deuteronomy 15:11. In traditional Christian teaching the evils of old age, the diseases and disabilities that afflict us, are consequences of our fallenness and participation in a fallen world, but old age itself is not an evil. It is part of the narrative of a created human life.

'Dependence is not an alien, subhuman, undignified condition; it is part of the narrative of every human life.'
(from talk)

Q3 What can we learn about God's plans for human beings from the Incarnation – the God who takes on human flesh and calls us into relationship with himself and with others?

In the Incarnation God chooses voluntarily to take on our human frailty and dependence, yet without sin. He demonstrates that dependence remains part of the divine plan for redeemed humanity, and that dependence does not in any way diminish our unique value, status and dignity as beloved children of the Most High.

Q4 In what practical ways could our local Christian community be better at mutual caring and burden-sharing? Are there good examples where this is already happening? Are there ways in which I could be more involved?

'We are dependent beings and to make independence our goal is to fly in the face of reality.'
Gilbert Meilaender

'I am designed to be a burden to you and you are designed to be a burden to me ... And the life of a family, including that of the local church, should be one of 'mutual burdensomeness.'"
(from talk)

Bible passages for reflection

Genesis 1:26-28

'Then God said, "Let us make man in our image, after our likeness. And let them have dominion over the fish of the sea and over the birds of the heavens and over the livestock and over all the earth and over every creeping thing that creeps on the earth."

So God created man in his own image, in the image of God he created him; male and female he created them. And God blessed them. And God said to them, "Be fruitful and multiply and fill the earth and subdue it, and have dominion over the fish of the sea and over the birds of the heavens and over every living thing that moves on the earth."'

Human beings are unique in the entire cosmos, as they were created by the Triune God to reflect his being and character, and to represent God within the created order. As God-like beings, humans are wonderful, unique and to be loved, respected and protected.

> 'Jesus was with us in the darkness of the womb as he will be with us in the darkness of the tomb.'
> Gilbert Meilaender

> 'If dependence is good enough for Jesus then perhaps it should be good enough for us.'
> Anon

Genesis 2:7

'…then the LORD God formed the man of dust from the ground and breathed into his nostrils the breath of life, and the man became a living creature.'

God has chosen to make us out of dust, out of the same stuff as everything else. And therefore we share the weakness, vulnerability and dependence of the rest of the physical creation.

Psalm 103:13,14

'As a father shows compassion to his children, so the LORD shows compassion to those who fear him. For he knows our frame; he remembers that we are dust.'

God's compassion and gentleness towards his children is based on his knowledge of our creation out of dust, and particularly our weakness, fragility and vulnerability.

Galatians 6:2

'Bear one another's burdens, and so fulfill the law of Christ.'

The bearing of burdens is intended to be reciprocal – we do this for one another – and it is part of our obedience to Christ.

Philippians 2:5-8

'Have this mind among yourselves, which is yours in Christ Jesus, who, though he was in the form of God, did not count equality with God a thing to be grasped, but emptied himself, by taking the form of a servant, being born in the likeness of men. And being found in human form, he humbled himself by becoming obedient to the point of death, even death on a cross.'

The wonderful example of Christ in emptying himself of his divine power and allowing himself to become dependent and vulnerable to the way he is treated and cared for by others. Paul uses Christ's example as a model for us to follow.

 Closing Prayer

Loving Father, we depend on You for everything! Thank You that Christ lived among us, sharing our human frailty and even dying on the cross. You care so much for those who are weak and suffering and send us out to support others with the skill and compassion You give. Amen.

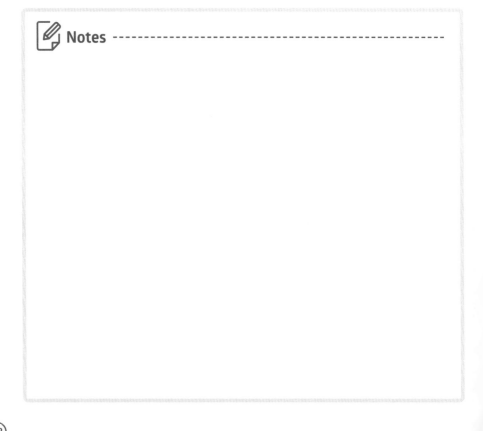

✎ Notes

3

Can suicide ever be a Christian way to die?

In this session we are focussing on the painful and disturbing topic of suicide. Some prominent voices are arguing that it can be an act of Christian compassion to help a terminally ill person kill themselves. But both the Bible and 2000 years of church teaching are opposed to suicide, seeing it not as a noble and responsible way to die, but as an act of despair and hopelessness.

It is important to remember that some group members may have been painfully affected in the past by the suicide of a family member or a close friend. It may be helpful to introduce the session by emphasising that this is a deeply personal and painful topic and to ask if members wish to share any personal experiences at the beginning. It is important to remember that episodes of despair and depression associated with suicidal thoughts are relatively common experiences amongst Christian believers, although this is rarely acknowledged.

💬 Text of the talk

'In today's discussion we will be focussing on the question of whether suicide can ever be seen as a good way to die, especially for a Christian believer. The topic of suicide is a deeply personal and painful one and I am conscious that there may be some people taking part in these discussions who have had personal experience. Maybe you have been affected by the tragedy of a loved-one who took their own life. Or maybe you yourself have faced periods of depression and despair and maybe you have contemplated taking your own life. Our hope and prayer is that these discussions may help us to address these painful and difficult issues and find practical ways forward.

Loving compassion

There are certainly some voices in today's world arguing that it might be an act of Christian compassion to help a terminally ill person to kill themselves. Lord Carey, the distinguished past Archbishop of Canterbury speaking in the House of Lords, said that he had changed his previous opposition to assisted suicide. These are his words, "When suffering is so great that some patients, already knowing that they are at the end of life, make repeated pleas to die, it seems a denial of that loving compassion which is the hallmark of Christianity to refuse to allow them to fulfil their own clearly stated request … If we truly love our neighbours as ourselves, how can we deny them the death that we would wish for ourselves in such a condition? That is what I would want…"

Lord Carey was arguing in favour of the proposed UK law which would allow a doctor to provide a lethal combination of medicines, drugs which are explicitly designed to kill, so that a patient with terminal illness might commit suicide. But can suicide, the deliberate destruction of one's own life, be an action that is consistent with the Christian faith? In many ancient cultures, suicide has been glorified as a noble way to die. The Norwegian warriors saw suicide as a path to heaven; in Japan, until recently, hari-kiri was seen as a noble form of death; in ancient Greece, the Stoics encouraged the heroic suicide.

Reaching out

But it's interesting that in all the cultures that have been influenced by Christianity, suicide has never been seen as noble or heroic. Certainly in the Bible, suicide is associated with despair and rebellion against God. Think for example of the tragic deaths of Saul and Judas Iscariot. Despite this, it seems that suicidal thoughts are not uncommon in God's people. Take Elijah – he wanted to die (It is enough Lord, take my life) but was sent on a sabbatical instead. Job wishes he had never been born, but learns that God is in control of his life. So God's people may at times be overwhelmed with grief or depression and they may wish to end their lives. I must be honest and say that I too went through a period

'Suicide is to throw your life away because there is nothing worth living for, it is an act of despair; martyrdom is to give your life because there is something even more wonderful to die for, it is an act of faith and hope' Anon

of deep depression some years ago and in that dark place I thought that maybe the best thing for everybody would be if could end my life. But I thank God that instead of helping me to kill myself, those around me responded and reached out with love, care and understanding, and I was able to find healing and recovery.

From a Christian understanding of the world, every human life is special and uniquely valuable, and therefore every

📝 **Notes** --

human life deserves protection. Joseph Pieper, a Christian philosopher, said this: 'Love is a way of saying to another person, "Its good that you are alive, it's good that you are in the world"'. But when we agree to help someone to kill themselves we are in effect saying "we think that your life is useless. We agree that it's bad that you are alive. It would be much better for the world if you didn't exist." But what right do we have to tell another person, made in God's image, that their life is worthless?

Respect and responsibility

Even when someone's life becomes restricted and limited by disease or disability, I do not think that we have the right to agree with them that their life is pointless. Not only is each human life uniquely precious and valuable. The Christian faith also teaches us that we are all part of the human family. We are created to be in community. Why do we try to prevent suicides in our society? Why are brave police officers expected to try to save the life of a man attempting to jump from a high bridge? It is because surprisingly our society, though penetrated by liberal individualism, is still deeply influenced by Christian thought. From a Christian perspective we are not autonomous individuals doing our own thing. We are locked together in community, bound together by duties of care, responsibility and compassion. Respect for human life, and the prohibition of suicide, is part of the glue which binds society together.

Although the act of self-destruction is often born out of desperation, loneliness and despair, suicide can have devastating effects on others. It seems almost as though the suicide strikes out at those who love them, wounding and damaging them, often for life. When someone I love chooses to kill themselves rather than carry on living, they often cause deep feelings of failure and grief. Perhaps I didn't love them enough. Perhaps I could have done more.

So I want to argue that the voices pressing in favour of helping suicides out of compassion are misguided. There must be a better way of caring for people at the end of their lives. Instead of changing the law to enable doctors to assist their patients to kill themselves, I think we need to learn what it means in practice to say to one another, "It's good that you are alive. It's good that you are in the world."

You know in the end suicide is always an act of despair and hopelessness. But as Christians we need to know that our life is never worthless and we have a hope that transcends the grave.

But maybe you disagree. In the next session we will be looking at a positive Christian understanding of what it means to die well and to die faithfully. But now is a chance to discuss some of painful issues that surround suicide using the questions in the booklet and the Bible passages for reflection.'

Q1 What are some of the reasons you think could drive people to suicide? Why do you think that suicide is never celebrated in the scriptures or in Christian history as a noble and godly way to die?

It is helpful to explore the underlying reasons why for the last 2000 years Christians have been opposed to suicide. These include a) our life is a gift from God, and our body is a temple of the Holy Spirit - we do not have the right to destroy it, b) the intentional destruction of innocent human life is against God's law, c) we cannot know what future plans God has for our lives, d) suicide causes profound and permanent damage to those who are closest to us, e) suicide damages the bonds of mutual care and support within our society.

Q2 How does suicide affect loved-ones, relatives and friends?

If no group member has had first hand experience the question might be rephrased: How do you think that suicide would affect loved-ones? etc

It is well known that suicide often causes very long-term psychological consequences for all. There may be feelings of guilt and failure – 'perhaps I could have done more, if only I had said something' etc. The discovery of the suicide is often traumatic and may leave long-term scars and painful memories. There may be feelings of anger, bitterness and resentment at the apparent 'selfishness' of the suicide.

> 'Love is a way of saying to a person it's good that you are alive, it's good that you are in the world'
> Joseph Pieper

Q3 Do you think it can ever be an act of compassion to help someone kill themselves, if they are desperate to die?

The critical issue here is the meaning of the word 'compassion'. There is no doubt that some people have assisted the suicide of a loved-one believing that they were acting compassionately, and this should be recognised. But in effect their action means that they were agreeing with the individual that their life was worthless. If Christian love is a way of saying to another person, 'It's good that you are alive, it's good that you are in the world' then it's hard to argue that assisting a suicide is consistent with this kind of love. The arguments outlined in Question 1 may be helpful here.

Q4 Is there a difference between suicide and martyrdom? – if so what is the difference?

In traditional Christian understanding there is a clear difference between suicide and martyrdom. Suicide is to kill yourself because there is nothing worth living for – it is an act of despair and hopelessness.

34

Martyrdom is to give your life because there is something even more valuable to die for – it is an act of faith, hope and love. It may be helpful to think of examples of martyrdom, either in Christian history or in the present, in order to illustrate the differences.

Q5 How would you respond practically if a close friend or relative expressed suicidal thoughts or was at risk of suicide?

A useful question to ask the individual is, 'Have you ever thought about harming yourself?'. If the person expresses suicidal thoughts it is generally accepted that it is morally and legally appropriate to break confidentiality in these circumstances because of the real risk to life. It is valuable to discuss what practical steps should be taken, particularly the importance of obtaining medical help rapidly in addition to pastoral and spiritual support. If the individual refuses to seek help it would be appropriate to offer to go with them to a medical appointment or emergency department.

 Notes --

 Bible passages for reflection

1 Corinthians 3:16,17

'Do you not know that you are God's temple and that God's Spirit dwells in you? If anyone destroys God's temple, God will destroy him. For God's temple is holy, and you are that temple.'

1 Corinthians 6:19,20

'Or do you not know that your body is a temple of the Holy Spirit within you, whom you have from God? You are not your own, for you were bought with a price. So glorify God in your body.'

These passages emphasise the dignity, significance, value and holiness of the human body.

Jeremiah 29:11

'"For I know the plans I have for you," declares the Lord, "plans for welfare and not for evil, to give you a future and a hope."'

Even the despairing believer can know that God has plans for his future welfare.

John 10:10

'The thief comes only to steal and kill and destroy. I came that they may have life and have it abundantly.'

Christ has come to bring life, not death.

'Suicide ... expresses a desire to be free but not also finite, a desire to be more like Creator than creature. .'
Gilbert Meilaender

Matthew 27:3-5

'Then when Judas, his betrayer, saw that Jesus was condemned, he changed his mind and brought back the thirty pieces of silver to the chief priests and the elders, saying, "I have sinned by betraying innocent blood." They said, "What is that to us? See to it yourself." And throwing down the pieces of silver into the temple, he departed, and he went and hanged himself.'

An illustration of suicide as an act of despair.

 ## Closing Prayer

Lord of all compassion, please draw near to anyone who is in such despair and pain that they are considering suicide. Grant wisdom and understanding to their families and friends, and to doctors, counsellors and others seeking to help them in this dark night of the soul. Please comfort those mourning for loved ones who have ended their lives. Amen.

Notes

4

Dying well and dying faithfully – personal aspects

Today's session provides an opportunity for us to reflect on what it means to die well and to die in a manner consistent with the Christian faith. Dying need not be a totally negative experience. As many who have gone before us have found, the end of our lives on this earth may be transformed by God's grace into an opportunity for growth and internal healing.

This session may allow an opportunity to explore the fears and anxieties that death brings, and the reality of the Christian hope. Although most Christian believers know the theory about hope and Christ's conquest of death, for many it is not an experienced reality.

🗪 Text of the talk

Running the race

'In today's discussion we will be focussing on the question of what it means to die well and to die faithfully as a Christian. This is not an easy topic and I am conscious of the fact that some people taking part in these discussions may find it painful and distressing. Perhaps it stirs up painful memories of watching a loved-one die, or perhaps you yourself are facing a terminal illness, and you are wondering what the future will hold.

The aim of these discussions is to provide a safe place, a framework in which these painful issues can be raised. As Christians we do not need to face death without hope. In the words of Psalm 23 "Even though I walk through the valley of the shadow of death, I will fear no evil, for you are with me; your rod and your staff, they comfort me."

The writer to the Hebrews tells us to "run with perseverance the race marked out for us", conscious of the fact that we are surrounded by witnesses, both our loved-ones and companions who are there with us – and an invisible cloud of faithful witnesses who have run this race before us.

Dying need not be a totally negative experience. It need not be all loss. In fact, it can even be a strange kind of adventure. As many who have gone before us have found, the end of our lives on this earth may be transformed by God's grace into an opportunity for growth and internal healing.

Personal examples

Today's session provides an opportunity for us to reflect on what it means to die well and in a manner consistent with the Christian faith. Perhaps you can give a personal example of a Christian believer known to you who died well. What can we learn from their example?

Many believers have found that dying well can be an opportunity for focussing on the things that really matter. A close friend of mine who found that he only had a few months to live decided that he would write a personal letter to everyone who had been significant in his life, sharing his heart and experiences, and his faith and hope in Christ. Many people received a letter and those last months turned into a rich and remarkable experience.

For others, the knowledge that life is drawing to an end gives an opportunity

> '...One short sleep past, we wake eternally,
> And death shall be no more; Death, thou shalt die.'
>
> John Donne

for fulfilling life-long dreams.

Dying well is also an opportunity for saying sorry and thank you to those who matter to us. It may be a once in a lifetime opportunity for reconciliation of relationships that have gone wrong, for sharing from the heart and for encouraging those who remain to serve faithfully. These conversations may not be easy but they can be some of the most significant and rewarding of our lifetime.

Important words

Here are some of the words and phrases we might use with those who are approaching the finishing line:

I love you …

I am praying for you …

Thank you …

Please forgive me …

I forgive you …

Is there anything you would like to say to me or to someone else?

I will walk this road with you to the end.

We will meet again.

Above all, those of us who remain are called to "be there" with the dying person. Words may not be important but our loving presence is. In my own experience, as I have had the opportunity of walking with those who are coming to the end of their earthly lives, I've discovered that there can be no higher privilege than just being there.

One of the difficult realities of modern society is that death has become a medical event. Dying has been taken over by the medics. Of course we want to benefit from the best in the way of pain relief and symptom control that modern

Notes

medicine can offer, but we need to emphasise that dying is really a spiritual event, even if it has medical implications. So the challenge we face is to ensure that where possible loved ones and the local community of believers are involved right up to the end.

Starting line

We are still called to walk the valley of the shadow of death, but we do it in the knowledge that God himself is with us. He too, in the person of Jesus has experienced death and he has defeated it. Death has lost its sting. In the New Testament it is very significant that believers are not described as "dying", instead they "fall asleep". The terror of death has been destroyed for ever in the resurrection life of Christ. The poet John Donne expressed it like this:

"One short sleep past, we wake eternally,

And death shall be no more; death, thou shalt die."

And so as we approach the finishing line, we see that line is the end of one form of existence, but it is actually the starting line of something far more wonderful.

As Paul says in 1 Corinthians: "What no eye has seen, what no ear has heard, what hasn't entered into the heart of mankind, God has prepared for those who love him.'"

$Q1$ **Can you think of any personal examples of a Christian believer who died well? What can we learn from their example? How is this different from a difficult or negative experience of death?**

It may be helpful to spend some time reflecting in depth on one or two personal examples.

$Q2$ **Do you think it is true that dying well can bring some kind of opportunities for blessing and healing? If so what are those opportunities – for the dying person, for those around them, and for the local church?**

Again, the aim should be to focus where possible on real life examples. If there are no such examples the question could be reframed , 'What do you imagine the opportunities of dying well might be?'

Some of the examples mentioned in the talk are:

Opportunities for:
- *focussing on the things that matter*
- *fulfilling life-long dreams*
- *saying sorry and thank you to those who matter to us*
- *reconciliation of relationships that have gone wrong*
- *sharing from the heart and for encouraging those who remain to serve faithfully*
- *prepare to meet our heavenly Father and his Son*

$Q3$ **Why do you think that people find it difficult to talk about how they would wish to die? What can we do to encourage more discussion about this topic within churches and with our loved ones?**

Rather than vague generalities, it may be helpful to encourage the group to give practical examples of ways that discussion could be encouraged within the local church community and in families.

Examples might be:
- *More emphasis on Bible teaching on death and dying*
- *Discussing and celebrating recent and historical examples of those who died well*
- *Using contemporary news stories about assisted suicide to start discussions with relatives and loved-ones*

 **Notes**

Bible passages for reflection

Hebrews 12:1,2

'Since we are surrounded by so great a cloud of witnesses, let us also lay aside every weight, and sin which clings so closely, and let us run with endurance the race that is set before us, looking to Jesus, the founder and perfecter of our faith, who for the joy that was set before him endured the cross, despising the shame, and is seated at the right hand of the throne of God.'

There is race to be run and it requires endurance, perseverance and single-mindedness, focusing on the example of Jesus. But we are surrounded by a great cloud of witnesses (both those on earth and those who have gone before) who are encouraging us on.

Psalm 23:6

'Even though I walk through the valley of the shadow of death, I will fear no evil, for you are with me; your rod and your staff, they comfort me.'

There is a deep mystery about death that we cannot penetrate, but the Shepherd promises to be with us all the way through the valley of the shadow of death.

John 11:25,26

'Jesus said to her, "I am the resurrection and the life. Whoever believes in me, though he die, yet shall he live, and everyone who lives and believes in me shall never die. Do you believe this?"'

Christian believers are promised that death is not the end. Death will be overcome by life. But there is a personal challenge to believe this truth and to live in the light of it.

'Suffering is not a question that demands an answer, it's not a problem that demands a solution, it's a mystery that demands a presence' Anon

The words of a dying person are important and should be treated with respect, especially if there is communication near the end. It is also important to remember that, when someone is dying, the sense of hearing may be retained long after other senses have gone. The person who appears to be unconscious and in a deep coma could still be able to hear, although they may be unable to respond physically. It is always important to talk to the person with sensitivity and caring, even though there appears to be no response. Here are some words and phrases that might be helpful:

'I love you'

Many of us find it hard to verbalise our deepest thoughts and feelings, but now is an opportunity for sharing from the heart.

'I am praying for you'

Many people at the end of life find it difficult to pray for themselves and assurance of prayers from others brings comfort.

'Thank you for...'

'Please forgive me for...'

Here is an opportunity for reconciliation and restoration of relationships that have become distorted and hurt.

'I forgive you'

'I will walk this road with you to the end.'

The greatest fear is often that of being abandoned and left alone as death approaches.

'We will meet again'

This is a reminder of the Christian hope – it is not the end of the story.

Closing Prayer

Jesus, our risen Saviour and faithful Friend, we are so grateful for the assurance that You will never forsake us and have gone ahead to prepare us a place in Heaven. Thank You for the remembrance of those we know who have died in the faith. Please comfort those nearing the end of their lives and grant them Your peace and confidence in Your promises. Amen.

Notes

5

Dying well and dying faithfully – medical and legal aspects

In today's discussion we continue the theme of what it means to die well and die faithfully – looking particularly at some medical and legal issues. There is evidence that some Christian believers insist on having every possible medical treatment right up to the moment of death – even if the treatment can bring no benefit. But why is this? Christian thinking about death always has a strange ambivalence. Death is not to be welcomed or hastened. Death is an evil, it is described as the last enemy. But although death is an enemy it can by God's grace turn into 'a severe mercy', even a strange form of healing, - a gateway to the new heaven and new earth.

👥💬 Text of the talk

'In today's discussion we continue the theme of what it means to die well and die faithfully – looking particularly at some medical and legal issues. One of the problems with modern society is that we have medicalised death and the process of dying. Death is something that happens in hospitals, when the constant struggle against disease is finally lost – dying has become a medical event. Death is what happens when the doctors run out of treatment options. You keep going for as long as possible. You have every treatment that's available but there comes a time when the doctors say, "We are very sorry but we have no other treatments left", then you die. Death becomes defined by what doctors can and cannot do.

Research findings

In 2009 a study of 300 patients with advanced and terminal cancer was carried out in the USA. The researchers assessed each patient's attitude to death and the extent to which religion was important to them in coping with their illness. The majority of them said they were Christians. The researchers then followed every patient over the last year of life until death. Paradoxically they found that those with "religious coping behaviour" was associated with increased preference for receiving all possible medical measures, and lower rates of making a "do not resuscitate" statement, or completing a living will. In the last week of life people with religious coping behaviour were more likely to die in an intensive care unit receiving full life support to the very end, compared with the others.

Why was this? The researchers found that religious people said that they believed that only God could decide when a patient should die, or they believed they had to carry on with maximal treatment in case God was going to do a miracle. Some said that accepting palliative care or stopping medical treatment meant "giving up on God". These results suggest that many believers think that they must have all possible treatments to the very end. But is dying in an intensive care unit with tubes coming out of every orifice really the best way that a Christian should die?

I think that Christian thinking about death always has a strange ambivalence. Death is not to be welcomed or hastened. Death is an evil, it is described as the last enemy. Human death is an outrage. Jesus himself weeps at the grave of Lazarus, even though he knows that the story has an unexpected ending. But although death is the final enemy it can on occasion by God's grace turn into a severe mercy, even

> 'You matter because you are you, and you matter to the end of your life. Not only will we help you die with dignity but we will help you to live before you die.'
> Cicely Saunders

a strange form of healing - a gateway to the new heaven and new earth.

Resurrection life

Jesus both shows us the importance of our current physical bodies but he also points to something that is even more important: the future resurrection life which is invading the present time. He

Notes --

Every medical treatment has potential benefits – it can bring good things – but everything the medics have to offer also carries burdens and risks. So we have to learn to balance the benefits of any treatment against its burdens. When a particular treatment leads to greater burdens than its benefits, then we should have the courage to say no. And saying no to burdensome or futile medical treatment is not a form of suicide or faithlessness, it is part of wise Christian living. So it is important to enter to into an open and honest discussion with medical and nursing caregivers – what are the possible treatments and what are their benefits and burdens?

shows us that our present limited physical existence is not the only or even the most important part of our lives. So Christians affirm the importance of physical healing, while recognizing that behind our physical experience there lies a deeper, richer, even more wonderful reality.

This means that we cannot make extending physical life by technology the ultimate aim of our lives. Sometimes we have to say no to medical progress. Sometimes we shall need the trust and the courage that enable us to decline what medical technology makes possible. And that's because this physical existence is not all there is; we need a deeper healing. So patients and doctors must know when to say "enough is enough".

Palliative care

The original vision behind modern palliative care was a Christian vision – a vision of practical and compassionate, skilled caring, to be a Christian presence for those dying of terminal illnesses.

Christian doctors in the 1950s and 60s were confronted with an appalling dilemma. There were growing numbers of older people who were dying slowly and painfully of cancer. And yet methods of pain relief were pretty limited. Should you watch them struggle and die in agony or should you kill them to put them out of their misery? What do you do when confronted with a choice between two evil alternatives? Well what happened is that some of those doctors invented a completely new way of caring – palliative care. The Christian doctor Cicely Saunders was a remarkable pioneer who invented a new way of caring for dying people, caring for the whole person. One of her slogans was "You don't have to kill the patient in order to kill the pain."

Cicely Saunders invented a way of caring that has gone around the world. Modern palliative care is a way of using specialised medical and nursing techniques, and a multidisciplinary team of carers, to treat the whole person in response to what she called the 'total pain' of dying. It is a way of helping dying people to make the most of their lives. Here's another of her quotes, 'You matter because you are you, and you matter to the end of your life. Not only will we help you to die in dignity, but we will help you to live before you die'.

Thinking ahead

The modern palliative care movement uses the concept of 'a good death' to encourage people to think ahead and make plans for how they would want to die. Talking frankly about the prospect of death can help avoid futile medical treatments and instead allow a comfortable, dignified and natural death. Key things to think about:

- Are there important things I want to accomplish before I die? Are there people to talk to, relationships to restore, affairs to set in order?

- What symptoms am I likely to suffer, and how can these be reduced? Talking to doctors and nurses specialising in palliative care can provide reassurance about the range of treatments that are available to ensure symptoms are well controlled.

- Where would I like to die? Although in reality many people die in hospital, most people when asked would prefer to die at home, or in a hospice. In many areas community palliative care teams exist to provide excellent end of life care.

- Who will support me spiritually? Good palliative care aims to support the whole person, and to address all forms of distress – physical, psychological and spiritual. Maintaining good pastoral care from friends at church or a trusted pastor or elder will be crucial in sustaining Christian faith as death approaches.

 **Notes** -----------------

The current legal framework in the UK is intended to ensure that, wherever possible, patients are fully involved in decisions about their medical care, and in whether they receive resuscitation in the event of a sudden medical deterioration or cardiac arrest. However, if patients become incapable of taking part in these decisions then everything that is decided by the healthcare team must be in that individual's "best interests".

Patients can make legally binding documents in advance to refuse invasive medical treatment if they become incapacitated. This is sometimes called a "living will". Alternatively you may appoint in advance one or more people to make medical and other care decisions on your behalf (called a lasting power of attorney).

Sometimes is may be helpful to write down a statement of your own values, a short document which expresses the things that matter most to you. The course booklet has a list of resources and websites that may be helpful.

Facing death has never been easy. But it's important to discuss these painful realities in advance with our loved ones and with those who are closest too us.

Hope and faith

Thank you for accompanying me over these five discussions. We are not alone in the Christian family and we are called to bear one another's burdens, to be there for one

'You don't have to kill the patient in order to kill the pain.'
Cicely Saunders

another and to say to each one, "it's good that you are alive". But most importantly, as we approach the finishing line, we need to reflect on the love of our Father from which nothing can separate us, on the risen Lord Jesus, the one who has destroyed the power of death, the Good Shepherd who has promised to walk with us through the valley of the shadow of death, and on the presence of the Holy Spirit who will continue to renew us inwardly, even as our outer body wastes away.

With the Christian community and the presence of the triune God we can die well and die faithfully. Hope is to hear the melody of the future – faith is to dance to that melody in the present.'

Some members of the group may have watched loved-ones die in the past in ways that were poorly controlled and distressing. These experiences may strongly colour their views about their own death. However, techniques of palliative care have significantly improved in the last decade or two and there is much greater awareness amongst health professionals of the importance of good care in the last days of life. Therefore previous painful experiences need not reflect the present reality.

Q1 Why do you think that some Christian believers insist on every possible medical treatment right up to the very end of life? What do you think are some of the reasons why it might be difficult sometimes to say 'enough is enough'? Can you think of any biblical material that would be relevant and helpful for this dilemma?

It seems that some Christians believe that if they do not have every possible medical treatment they are in some way devaluing their own life, or colluding with some form of mercy killing. Other Christians believe that they are giving every opportunity for God to perform a miracle of healing and that by not having every possible treatment they may be guilty of "lack of faith". Sometimes it is an unspoken fear of death that drives patients or relatives to request every possible treatment, whatever the side effects might be.

Biblical material that might be relevant includes: 2 Tim 4:6-8 and Philippians 1:21-23 below. Other passages include Romans 14:8, 2 Corinthians 5:1-8, and 1 Corinthians 15:42-49.

Q2 How can we know when 'enough is enough' and that treatment should stop?

This is a very personal and difficult question and there are no "right" answers. It seems that God gives to us the dignity of freedom to choose what is wise and right for us – and different people will come to different conclusions. Some believers wish to receive potentially curative treatment right to the end, whereas others, once they know that natural death is inevitable, wish to refuse all curative treatment, receiving only medication for pain relief and symptom control. In principle we should only receive a particular treatment if the potential benefits of that treatment outweigh its burdens and risks.

The next three questions deal with specific personal details about how we would like to die. Of course they are not easy questions to answer but it is helpful for all of us to start reflecting on the issues. Some group members may find these questions too personal or painful and there should be no pressure to contribute. It may be less uncomfortable to discuss the questions as generalities. For example 'Where do you think it is best for most people to die?'

Q3 How and where would you most prefer to die? Who would you ideally wish to be there with you? What treatments (if any) would you like to continue?

Most people would prefer to die at home in familiar circumstances, although some feel more secure in a hospice or hospital environment. Reflection on who we would wish to be with us is valuable because it may highlight the relationships that are most significant to us. Many people worry about the possibility of abandonment by others as the finishing line approaches. The question about treatments helps to focus attention on what different medical treatments are intending to achieve. If death is inevitable it may be wise to stop all medical treatment except those that help pain relief and symptom control.

Q4 If on medication, would you like to be able to communicate with your loved-ones and carers or would you prefer to be drowsy and sleepy as the end approaches?

It is often fear that drives patients or relatives to request increasing amounts of sedative or sleep-inducing medicine as the end approaches. Yet in many cases, with expert medical and nursing care it is possible to remain conscious and responsive without suffering significant pain or discomfort. It may be helpful to refer to the biblical promises that neither death nor life nor anything else can separate us from the love of God that is in Christ Jesus our Lord (Romans 8:38,39)

Q5 What would you like to communicate to the medical team and other carers in the last days about your care, treatment and decision-making, if you were unable to communicate in person?

It is helpful for group members to reflect on their own personal priorities in the last days. How might the medical and nursing care be tailored to help individuals achieve their own priorities? Include spiritual and pastoral needs in the discussion. A written personal 'statement of values' can be of assistance in setting out an individual's priorities and concerns. It may be helpful to point members to other resources listed in the booklet and elsewhere that may assist.

 **Bible passages for reflection**

2 Timothy 4:6-8

'For I am already being poured out as a drink offering, and the time of my departure has come. I have fought the good fight, I have finished the race, I have kept the faith. Henceforth there is laid up for me the crown of righteousness, which the Lord, the righteous judge, will award to me on that day, and not only to me but also to all who have loved his appearing.'

Paul is facing his death with faith. He looks back to the race that he has run, and looks forward to meeting the Lord, together with all the others who have travelled the same journey.

Our resurrection hope is based on the unassailable fact that the Redeemer lives. Even though our old bodies are destroyed we shall receive new bodies and we ourselves shall see God.

1 Corinthians 15:42-44

'So is it with the resurrection of the dead. What is sown is perishable; what is raised is imperishable. It is sown in dishonour; it is raised in glory. It is sown in weakness; it is raised in power. It is sown a natural body; it is raised a spiritual body.'

Our old bodies are like seed that has to die. Our wonderful new bodies will be raised imperishable, glorious, powerful, inspired and transformed by the Holy Spirit.

Philippians 1: 21-23

'For to me, to live is Christ and to die is gain. But if I am to live on in the flesh, this will mean fruitful labour for me; and I do not know which to choose. But I am hard-pressed from both directions, having the desire to depart and be with Christ, for that is very much better…'

To die is not loss but gain, to be with Christ which is much better than our earthly existence.

'Hope is to hear the melody of the future: Faith is to dance to that melody in the present.'
Anon

Job 19:25-27

'For I know that my Redeemer lives, and at the last he will stand upon the earth.

And after my skin has been thus destroyed, yet in my flesh I shall see God,

whom I shall see for myself, and my eyes shall behold, and not another.

My heart faints within me!'

Closing Prayer

God of all hope, please give us wisdom and courage to think about the 'finishing line' of our own lives. Thank You for every provision of care, palliative treatments and other support available to us and those close to us. I trust You, Lord, that at the end You will be our comforting and peaceful presence. Amen

Resources for further reading and support

Official Government information on lasting power of attorney
www.gov.uk/power-of-attorney/overview

NHS information on advance decision to refuse treatment
www.nhs.uk/Planners/end-of-life-care/Pages/advance-decision-to-refuse-treatment.aspx

National Council for Palliative Care - the umbrella charity for all those involved in palliative, end of life and hospice care in England, Wales and Northern Ireland.
www.ncpc.org.uk

Dying Matters – a secular organisation which aims to help people talk more openly about dying, death and bereavement, and to make plans for the end of life.
www.dyingmatters.org/overview/about-us

Books

Matters of Life and Death, John Wyatt, InterVarsity Press

The Art of Dying, Living Fully into the Life to Come, Rob Moll, InterVarsity Press

Living Well and Dying Faithfully: Christian Practices for End-of-Life Care, John Swinton, Eerdmans

Facing serious illness
Christian Medical Fellowship

The Human Journey, Peter Saunders, Christian Medical Fellowship

Code Red, Andrew Drain, Christian Medical Fellowship

Tracing the Rainbow - Walking Through Loss and Bereavement, Pablo Martinez, IVP

Right to Die – John Wyatt, InterVarsity Press (in press)

Organisations

CARE
www.care.org.uk

Christian Medical Fellowship
www.cmf.org.uk

Care Not Killing
www.carenotkilling.org.uk